I0409675

Typed Resource Definitions

Search and Rescue Resources

FEMA 508-8

November 2005

Background | The National Mutual Aid and Resource Management Initiative supports the National Incident Management System (NIMS) by establishing a comprehensive, integrated national mutual aid and resource management system that provides the basis to type, order, and track all (Federal, State, and local) response assets.

Resource Typing | For ease of ordering and tracking, response assets need to be categorized via resource typing. Resource typing is the categorization and description of resources that are commonly exchanged in disasters via mutual aid, by capacity and/or capability. Through resource typing, disciplines examine resources and identify the capabilities of a resource's components (i.e., personnel, equipment, training). During a disaster, an emergency manager knows what capability a resource needs to have to respond efficiently and effectively. Resource typing definitions will help define resource capabilities for ease of ordering and mobilization during a disaster. As a result of the resource typing process, a resource's capability is readily defined and an emergency manager is able to effectively and efficiently request and receive resources through mutual aid during times of disaster.

Web Site | For more information, you can also refer to the National Mutual Aid and Resource Management Web site located at:

http://www.fema.gov/nims/mutual_aid.shtm.

Supersedure | This document replaces *Search and Rescue Resources*, dated May 2005

Changes | Changed the name of the Swiftwater/Flood Search and Dive Rescue Team to Swiftwater/Flood Search and Rescue Team. Also added a reference source to the *Comments* section.

Table of Contents

RESOURCE:	Air Search Team (Fixed-Wing)				
CATEGORY:	Search & Rescue (ESF #9)			KIND:	Team

MINIMUM CAPABILITIES:						
COMPONENT	METRIC	TYPE I	TYPE II	TYPE III	TYPE IV	OTHER
Vehicle	Fixed-Wing Aircraft	Same as Type II	IFR Capable Fixed-Wing Observation Aircraft	Same as Type IV	Fixed-Wing Observation Aircraft	
Vehicle	Capacity	4-8 passengers with cargo not to exceed design specification of aircraft	Same as Type III	Same as Type IV	2-4 passenger with cargo not to exceed design specification of aircraft	
Equipment	Flight Suit	Same as Type II	Same as Type III	Same as Type IV	Appropriate level of PPE	
Equipment	Communications	Same as Type II except: Satellite Phone	Same as Type III	Same as Type IV except: VHF Radios	Standard FAA FM Radio	
Equipment	Video/Electronic	Same as Type III except: Capable of Airborne Video Transmission	Same as Type III except: Capable of flying back video or still imagery	Electronic Direction Finding Capable	None	
Aircrews	Training & Ratings	Pilot – Commercial (instrument) or higher certificate and complete unit certification program. Observer – Complete unit certification program	Pilot – Private Pilot (instrument) or higher certificate and complete unit certification program. Observer – Complete unit certification program	Same as Type IV	Pilot – Private Pilot or higher certificate and complete unit certification program. Observer – Complete unit certification program	
Aircrews	Crew Availability	Aircrew(s) available for extended operations	Aircrew(s) available for 8 to 14 days of operations	Aircrew(s) available for 3 to 7 days of operations	Aircrew(s) available for at least 2 days of operations	
Management Support	Overhead Incident Management	Full incident command staff capable of managing all phases of air search operations	Incident staff capable of managing air operations branch	Incident staff capable of supporting independent flight release	Unit level flight release; No search management capabilities	

COMMENTS:	Aircrews can work a maximum of 12-hour shifts, depending on individual unit policies and procedures. Aircraft will be maintained in accordance with Federal Aviation Administration Regulations. Aircraft will be expected to operate out of established airfield with paved runways. Aircrews will indicate fueling and runway requirements for the aircraft provided. Crew availability does not require continuous availability of specific personnel, only that crews are available to those specifications.

RESOURCE:		Airborne Reconnaissance (Fixed-Wing)				
CATEGORY:	Search & Rescue (ESF #9)			KIND:	Team	
MINIMUM CAPABILITIES:						
COMPONENT	METRIC	TYPE I	TYPE II	TYPE III	TYPE IV	OTHER
Vehicle	Fixed-Wing Aircraft	Same as Type II	IFR Capable Fixed-Wing Observation Aircraft	Same as Type IV	Fixed-Wing Observation Aircraft	
Vehicle	Capacity	4-8 passengers with cargo not to exceed design specification of aircraft	Same as Type III	Same as Type IV	2-4 passengers with cargo not to exceed design specification of aircraft	
Equipment	Flight Suit	Same as Type II	Same as Type III	Same as Type IV	Appropriate level of PPE	
Equipment	Communications	Same as Type II except: Satellite Phone	Same as Type III	Same as Type IV except: VHF Radios	Standard FAA FM Radio	
Equipment	Video/Electronic	Capable of flying back video or still imagery Capable of High Resolution Airborne Video Transmission Desired: FLIR or other infrared capabilities Desired: Capable of supporting Hyperspectral Imaging Requests	Same as Type III except: Capable of Low resolution Airborne Video Transmission Desired: FLIR or other infrared capabilities	Capable of flying back video or still imagery	None	
Personnel	Training & Ratings	Pilot – Commercial (instrument) or higher certificate and complete unit certification program Observer – Complete unit certification program	Pilot – Private Pilot (instrument) or higher certificate and complete unit certification program Observer – Complete unit certification program	Same as Type IV	Pilot – Private Pilot or higher certificate and complete unit certification program Observer – Complete unit certification program	
Personnel	Crew Availability	Aircrew(s) available for extended operations	Aircrew(s) available for 8 to 14 days of operations	Aircrew(s) available for 3 to 7 days of operations	Aircrew(s) available for at least 2 days of operations	
Management Support	Overhead Incident Management	Full Incident Command staff capable of managing all phases of air search operations	Incident staff capable of managing air operations branch	Incident staff capable of supporting independent flight release	Unit level flight release; no incident management capabilities	

FEMA

RESOURCE:	Airborne Reconnaissance (Fixed-Wing)			
CATEGORY:	Search & Rescue (ESF #9)		KIND:	Team
MINIMUM CAPABILITIES:	TYPE I	TYPE II	TYPE III	TYPE IV	OTHER
COMPONENT	METRIC			
COMMENTS:	Aircrews can work a maximum of 12-hour shifts, depending on individual unit policies and procedures. Aircraft will be maintained in accordance with Federal Aviation Administration Regulations. Aircraft will be expected to operate out of established airfield with paved runways. Aircrews will indicate fueling and runway requirements for the aircraft provided. Crew availability does not require continuous availability of specific personnel, only that crews are available to those specifications.			

FEMA

U.S. Department of Homeland Security
Federal Emergency Management Agency

RESOURCE:	Canine Search and Rescue Team – Avalanche Snow Air Scent				
CATEGORY:	Search & Rescue (ESF #9)		**KIND:** Team		
MINIMUM CAPABILITIES:					
COMPONENT	METRIC	TYPE I	TYPE II	TYPE III	TYPE IV	OTHER
Personnel	Dog Team	1 Dog 1 Handler 1 Support Person	Same as Type I			
Equipment	Search Capabilities	Capable of self-sustaining and searching for 24 hours in extreme weather and terrain conditions through avalanche debris fields	Capable of self-sustaining and searching for 24 hours in snow-covered environments in extreme weather conditions and moderate terrain			
Personnel	Equipment	Personal snow travel equipment and gear to self-sustain for 24 hours Equipped to include cross-country skis or snow shoes, poles, probe poles, snow shovel, and avalanche beacon	Same as Type I			
Personnel	Training	Training, including avalanche safety and winter survival, including building snow cave, First Aid for both human and dog, personal/ dog safety, and radio communications	Same as Type I			
COMMENTS:	**Note:** Many of these resources are capable of searching in a disaster environment, such as a wilderness team in outlying areas of a tornado zone, etc. It is critical that canine management personnel, knowledgeable in multiuse of canine resources, are available to Incident Command. This will not necessarily be reflected in this document.				

FEMA 508-8 Typed Resource Definitions - Search and Rescue Resources
11/14/2005

RESOURCE:	Canine Search and Rescue Team – Disaster Response				
CATEGORY:	Search & Rescue (ESF #9)		KIND:	Team	
MINIMUM CAPABILITIES:					
COMPONENT	METRIC	TYPE I	TYPE II	TYPE III	TYPE IV	OTHER
Personnel	Dog Team	1 Dog 1 Handler 1 Support Person				
Personnel	Search Capabilities	A disaster search canine that has successfully completed the DHS/FEMA Disaster Search Canine Readiness Evaluation for both Type II and Capable of national and international responses	A disaster search canine that has successfully completed the DHS/FEMA Disaster Search Canine Readiness Evaluation for Type II only; Capable of national and international responses	A disaster search canine that has successfully completed Disaster Search Canine Readiness Evaluation through an organized disaster task force – non-FEMA; Capable of national and international responses	A search canine with minimal exposure to disaster search; Capable of local/regional response only; No task force participation	
Team	Knowledge and Equipment	All requirements as set forth by DHS/FEMA National US&R Response System	All requirements as set forth by DHS/FEMA National US&R Response System	All requirements as set forth by organized task force for availability for national/international response	Agility; Obedience; First Aid-Human/Dog; HazMat; Disaster; Environment Exposure minimal; Initial responder readiness through local agency	
COMMENTS:	Please note that many of these resources are capable of searching in a disaster environment, such as a wilderness team in outlying areas of a tornado zone, etc. It is critical that canine management personnel, knowledgeable in multiuse of canine resources, are available to Incident Command. This will not necessarily be reflected in this document.					

Canine Search and Rescue Team – Land Cadaver Air Scent

RESOURCE:						
CATEGORY:	Search & Rescue, Other			**KIND:**	Team	
MINIMUM CAPABILITIES:						
COMPONENT	**METRIC**	**TYPE I**	**TYPE II**	**TYPE III**	**TYPE IV**	**OTHER**
Personnel	Dog Team	1 Dog 1 Handler 1 Support Person	Same as Type I	Same as Type I	Same as Type I	Same as Type I
Team	Search Capabilities	Capable of locating less than 15 grams of human remains during disaster ops; Capable of self-sustaining for 24 hours	Capable of locating deceased persons (greater than 15 grams) in disaster ops; Capable of self-sustaining for 24 hours	Capable of locating less than 15 grams of human remains buried, hanging, ground level, or in vehicles, nondisaster	Capable of locating less than 15 grams of human remains buried, hanging, ground level, nondisaster	Capable of locating deceased persons (greater than 15 grams) buried, hanging, ground level, nondisaster
Team	Knowledge and Equipment	Same as Type II	Same as Type III plus: Disaster ops training and capabilities	Same as Type IV	Training and equipment for biohazard environment, including OSHA guidelines, scene preservation, documentation, collection, chain of custody, and scene security First Aid for both human and dog, personal/ dog safety, and radio communications	Same as Type IV
COMMENTS:						

FEMA

RESOURCE:	Canine Search and Rescue Team – Water Air Scent				
CATEGORY:	Search & Rescue (ESF #9)		KIND:	Team	

MINIMUM CAPABILITIES:						
COMPONENT	METRIC	TYPE I	TYPE II	TYPE III	TYPE IV	OTHER
Personnel	Dog Team	1 Dog 1 Handler 1 Support Person				
Team	Search Capabilities	Capable of working swiftwater/stillwater environments; Trained and equipped to perform search ops on foot and from any type of watercraft	Capable of working stillwater environments; Trained and equipped to perform search ops on foot and from any type of watercraft	Capable of working swiftwater and stillwater ops from shore only	Capable of working swiftwater ops from shore only	Type V capable of working stillwater ops from shore only Type VI capable of working salt-water and very large fresh water environments from both boat and shore Type VII capable of working salt-water and very large fresh water environments from shore only
Team	Knowledge and Equipment	Water Helmet; Class V Water Vest; Throw Rope Swiftwater lifesaving skills; Knowledge of water rescue and boat operations; First Aid for both human and dog; Personal/dog safety Radio communications	Water Helmet; Class III-V Water Vest; Throw Rope Stillwater lifesaving skills; Knowledge of water rescue operations in stillwater environment; First Aid for both human and dog; Personal/dog safety Radio communications equipment	Same as Type I	Same as Type I	Type V same as Type II Type VI, VII same as Type I

COMMENTS:	Note: Many of these resources are capable of searching in a disaster environment, such as a wilderness team in outlying areas of a tornado zone, etc. It is critical that canine management personnel, knowledgeable in multiuse of canine resources, are available to Incident Command. This will not necessarily be reflected in this document.

U.S. Department of Homeland Security
Federal Emergency Management Agency

RESOURCE:	Canine Search and Rescue Team – Wilderness Air Scent				
CATEGORY:	Search & Rescue (ESF #9)			**KIND:** Team	

MINIMUM CAPABILITIES:						
COMPONENT	METRIC	TYPE I	TYPE II	TYPE III	TYPE IV	OTHER
Single Resource	Search Capabilities	Capable of search and self-sustaining for 72 hours in all weather and low angle wilderness terrain or larger areas of 60+ acres	Capable of searching and self-sustaining for 48 hours in all weather and low angle wilderness terrain or larger areas of 60+ acres	Capable of searching high probability local wilderness terrain for short durations (24 hours or less) or small areas 40-60 acres	Capable of searching high probability local wilderness terrain for short durations (12 hours or less) or small areas 40-60 acres	Human discriminating (scent source necessary)
Single Resource	Search Capabilities	Capable of searching and self-sustaining for 72 hours in all weather and low angle wilderness terrain or larger areas of 120+ acres	Capable of searching and self-sustaining for 48 hours in all weather and low angle wilderness terrain or larger areas of 120+ acres	Capable of searching high probability local wilderness terrain for short durations (24 hours or less) or small areas of 60-120 acres	Capable of searching high probability local wilderness terrain for short durations (12 hours or less) or small areas of 40-60 acres	Non-discriminating (locate all human indication in area)

COMMENTS:	There are significant differences in the training required for urban versus wilderness environments, both in air scent/area and trailing/tracking. Because of the vast differences, often a resource highly skilled in one environment may not function as well in the other environment because of a lack of continuous training in the environment. Teams may be cross-trained in both environments, depending on the team training criteria.
	Note: Many of these resources are capable of searching in a disaster environment, such as a wilderness team in outlying areas of a tornado zone, etc. It is critical that canine management personnel, knowledgeable in multiuse of canine resources, are available to Incident Command. This will not necessarily be reflected in this document.

RESOURCE:		Canine Search and Rescue Team – Wilderness Tracking/Trailing				
CATEGORY:		Law Enforcement/Security, Search & Rescue (ESF #9)		KIND:	Team	
MINIMUM CAPABILITIES:		TYPE I	TYPE II	TYPE III	TYPE IV	OTHER
COMPONENT	METRIC					
Personnel	Dog Team	Same as Type IV	Same as Type IV	Same as Type IV	1 Dog 1 Handler 1 Support Person	Same as Type IV
Team	Search Capabilities	Capable of trailing in wilderness terrain Aged 24+ hours; 1 mile or longer; Heavy contamination	Capable of trailing in wilderness terrain Aged 4-12 hours; 1 mile or longer; Heavy contamination	Capable of trailing in wilderness terrain Aged 1.5-4 hours; .5-1 mile; Heavy contamination	Capable of trailing in wilderness terrain Aged 0-1.5 hours; .25-.5 mile; Heavy contamination	Discriminating (scent source must be available)
Personnel	Equipment	Personally equipped for 24 hours for dog/handler First Aid for both human and dog Radio communications	Same as Type I	Same as Type I	Same as Type I	N/A
Personnel	Knowledge	Wilderness survival skills Capable of establishing and maintaining direction of travel First Aid for both human and dog Personal/ dog safety Skill in collection of scent articles	Same as Type I	Same as Type I	Same as Type I	N/A
COMMENTS:		As these dogs use scent articles, they are commonly referred to as trailing dogs. However, occasionally, a unit may refer to such dogs as tracking dogs. They do have the capability of human discrimination between sources with the aid of a provided scent source. Care should be taken to determine if a tracking dog requires the use of an article or not. **Note:** Many of these resources are capable of searching in a disaster environment, such as a wilderness team in outlying areas of a tornado zone, etc. It is critical that canine management personnel, knowledgeable in multiuse of canine resources, are available to Incident Command. This will not necessarily be reflected in this document.				

U.S. Department of Homeland Security
Federal Emergency Management Agency

RESOURCE:		Cave Search and Rescue Team				
CATEGORY:	Search & Rescue (ESF #9)			KIND:	Team	
MINIMUM CAPABILITIES:		TYPE I	TYPE II	TYPE III	TYPE IV	OTHER
COMPONENT	METRIC					
Team	Personnel	Same as Type III	Same as Type III	Same as Type IV plus Medical specialist	Field team leader Field team members	
Personnel	Cave Training	Same as Type II, plus: Proficiency in cave and surface search; Proficiency in high- and low-angle technical rescues and evacuations from dry, wet, and multidrop caves	Same as Type III, plus: Proficiency in vertical environments greater than 100 feet in depth; Ability to safely traverse multidrop caves; Ability to rapidly ascend a rope next to a litter during a litter raise	Same as Type IV, plus: Ability to carry additional rescue-related equipment to and through the cave	Basic understanding of the cave environment, including regional differences in ambient cave temperature, normal hazards such as risk of flooding, hypothermia, and potential changes in cave environment because of seasonal variations and outside weather; Proficiency in crawling, climbing and moving over uneven surfaces and breakdown areas covered in mud, sand, or water; Familiarity with chimneying, bridging, and other basic climbing techniques used in moving through caves; Ability to move comfortably and efficiently in small spaces; Ability to rappel and ascend 66' of static line using standard single rope techniques; Proficiency in changing over from ascent to rappel and rappel to ascent; Ability to carry personal	

Cave Search and Rescue Team

RESOURCE:						
CATEGORY: Search & Rescue (ESF #9)				**KIND:** Team		
MINIMUM CAPABILITIES:						
COMPONENT	**METRIC**	**TYPE I**	**TYPE II**	**TYPE III**	**TYPE IV**	**OTHER**
					equipment to and through the cave; Ability to identify fragile cave environments and take measures to protect them; Ability to maintain primary light sources	
					Familiar with cave maps and topographic maps	
Personnel	Navigation Training	Same as Type II	Same as Type III, plus: Proficiency in back-country navigation and route finding with a map and compass, use of GPS and UTM coordinate system	Same as Type IV, plus: Knowledge of common symbols present on cave maps; Proficiency in reading cave maps; Ability to use topographic maps to locate caves		
Personnel	Basic Training	Same as Type II, plus; Ability to plan, organize, and direct cave rescue and search missions using ICS; Experience with ICS Unified Command	Same as Type III, plus: Ability to direct activities according to ICS; Technical proficiency in single person rope rescue techniques; Proficiency in crack and crevice rescue; Proficiency in creating load distributing and artificial anchors in-cave	Same as Type IV, plus: Capable of operating within ICS; Proficiency in edge tending for the vertical environment; Proficiency in preparing and rigging basket and flexible litters for haul and lower operations; Proficiency in patient packaging for extrication; Familiarity with the basic techniques for crack and crevice rescue; Ability to improvise patient packaging	Familiarity with basic cave search techniques; Familiarity with the NIIMS ICS of incident management; Proficiency in establishing simple anchors and fixing lines for personal rappels and ascents; Awareness of the psychological and physical patient considerations in rescue extrications of long duration; Proficiency in basic in-cave litter movement techniques; Ability to assist in patient packaging for extrication; Specialized training required	

RESOURCE:		Cave Search and Rescue Team			
CATEGORY:	Search & Rescue (ESF #9)		**KIND:**	Team	
MINIMUM CAPABILITIES:					
COMPONENT	**METRIC**	**TYPE I**	**TYPE II**	**TYPE III**	**TYPE IV**	**OTHER**

COMPONENT	METRIC	TYPE I	TYPE II	TYPE III	TYPE IV	OTHER
					to safely and appropriately use communication and technical rescue equipment	
Personnel	Technical Training	Same as Type II, plus: Proficiency in the use, placement, and analysis of mechanical anchors and anchor systems; Proficiency in use of highlines and guiding lines; Proficiency in the organization and direction of technical cave rescue searches and rescues; For regions/caves with swiftwater: Proficiency in working in and around moving water underground; Swiftwater/flatwater technician For regions/caves with bad air: Proficiency in the use of a 3-gas monitor (oxygen, hydrogen sulfide and carbon monoxide) and ability to understand its output	Same as Type III, plus: Understanding of the mechanical forces involved in technical rescue systems; Proficiency in the selection and setup of rescue anchor systems; Proficiency at estimating component and system load ratios and assessing safety factors; Ability to rig and operate simple and compound 4:1, 6:1, and 9:1 mechanical advantage systems; Proficiency in rigging and use of counterbalance systems; Proficiency in technical litter evacuations and transport including litter raises and lowers on breakdown, in free-fall and other vertical environments, in narrow or waterfall situations, and in multidrop caves	Same as Type IV, plus: Proficiency in tying common knots and knowledge of their applications and strength efficiencies; Proficiency in establishing simple anchors for haul and lower systems; Ability to establish 2:1 and 3:1 haul systems, fixed brake lowering systems, and belay systems; Familiarity with basic search techniques and nomenclature; Ability to maintain scene integrity in case of crime; Proficiency in establishing and operating in-cave wired communications systems; Ability to operate a handheld radio; Proficiency in choosing appropriate in-cave litter movement techniques	Ability to serve as a member of a haul or lower team and familiarity of appropriate commands; Ability to serve as a member of an evacuation team; Other skills or abilities as identified by the team's operations leader	
Personnel	Survival Training	Same as Type III	Same as Type III	Same as Type IV, plus: Experience in wet and vertical caves	Operational proficiency in the cave environment for the region	

Cave Search and Rescue Team

RESOURCE:						
CATEGORY:	Search & Rescue (ESF #9)			**KIND:**	Team	
MINIMUM CAPABILITIES:						
COMPONENT	**METRIC**	**TYPE I**	**TYPE II**	**TYPE III**	**TYPE IV**	**OTHER**
Personnel	Medical Specialist Training	National Standard EMT-B, with BTLS or PHTLS	National Standard EMT-B, or advanced wilderness first responder; BTLS	Same as Type IV	Basic First Aid/CPR	
Team	Sustained Operations	48 hours or more	36 hours	24 hours	24 hours	
Team	Search and Rescue Capabilities	Same as Type II with experience complex rescue environments as appropriate for region of activity	Same as Type III with experience in wet and vertical caves and crack/crevice situations	Same as Type IV	Trained cave rescue and cave search personnel with experience in relatively dry caves with moderate vertical situations	
Equipment	Team Supplies and Materials	Same as Type III, plus: Ability to support more than 2 patients at 2 separate incidents; Sufficient rope and hardware to support complex rigging, multiple drops, highline, etc. In regions/caves with swiftwater: Appropriate floatation equipment for patient(s) and other necessary swiftwater-specific rigging equipment In regions/caves with bad air: 3-gas monitors	Same as Type III, plus: Ability to respond to two in-cave patients simultaneously	Same as Type IV, plus:	Harnesses, Helmets; Basic hardware (including: 7/16 or .5" static kernmantle rope, webbing, pulleys, carabiners, lowering devices, etc.) Field telephones and wire Radio communications on a common frequency Patient packaging materials Litters appropriate for situation Entrance control materials; Edge protection	
Equipment	Personal Supplies and materials	Same as Type II, plus: Food for 48 hours In regions/caves with swiftwater: Appropriate swiftwater gear, PFD, personal throwbags,	Same as Type III, plus: Food for 36 hours	Same as Type IV, plus: Wetsuit where appropriate	Personal protective equipment including: Footwear, underwear, and outerwear suited to the particular cave environment Sewn seat harness; Personal	

Cave Search and Rescue Team

RESOURCE:					
CATEGORY:	Search & Rescue (ESF #9)		**KIND:**	Team	

MINIMUM CAPABILITIES:

COMPONENT	METRIC	TYPE I	TYPE II	TYPE III	TYPE IV	OTHER
		and waterproof light sources			descending and ascending equipment with 2 points of attachment above the waist	
					Helmet (with 3- or 4-point chinstrap suspension system); Gloves with leather palms	
					3 independent sources of light, each capable of exiting the cave; 2 of which must be helmet-mountable	
					Batteries (carbide if appropriate)	
					Quantity of water appropriate for the conditions	
					Food for 24 hours	
					Knife/multitool	
					Personal first aid kit	
					Waterproof pen/pencil and paper	
					Appropriate pack to carry personal gear; food for 24 hours	
Equipment	Medical Supplies and Materials	Same as Type IV	Same as Type IV	Same as Type IV	As appropriate for level of training, as applied in wilderness/cave environment and meeting local protocols and requirements	

COMMENTS:

RESOURCE:		Collapse Search and Rescue Teams				
CATEGORY:	Search & Rescue		KIND:	Team		
MINIMUM CAPABILITIES:						
COMPONENT	METRIC	TYPE I	TYPE II	TYPE III	TYPE IV	OTHER
Personnel	Training and Certification	Trained to the HazMat Technician Level (NFPA 472) Comply with NFPA 1006 Technician Level requirements for their area of specialization or organization Operations Level for support personnel as outlined in NFPA 1670.	Trained to the HazMat First Responder Operational Level (NFPA 472) Comply with organization Operations Level for support personnel as outlined in NFPA 1670.	Trained to the HazMat First Responder Operational Level (NFPA 472) Comply with organization Operations Level for support personnel as outlined in NFPA 1670	Trained to HazMat First Responder Awareness Level (NFPA 472) Comply with organization Awareness Level for support personnel as outlined in NFPA 1670	
Team	Training	Trained for Heavy Floor Construction, Pre-cast Concrete Construction, Steel Frame Construction, High Angle Rope Rescue (including highline systems), Confined Space Rescue (permit required), and Mass Transportation Rescue	Trained for Heavy Wall Construction, High Angle Rope Rescue (not including highline systems), Confined Space (no permit required) and Trench and Excavation Rescue	Trained for Light Frame Construction and Low Angle Rope Rescue	Trained for Surface Rescue and Non-Structural Entrapment in Non-Collapsed Structures	
Team	Sustained Operations	Capable of sustained heavy operations for 18-24 hours	Medium operations for 12-24 hours Typically require relief for sustained 24-hour operations	Light operations for 6-12 hours Typically require assistance from additional team for sustained 12-hour operations	Basic operations for 3-6 hours Typically require assistance for sustained 6-hour operations	
Team	Safe and Effective Response Operation Incidents	Conduct safe and rescue operations at incidents involving collapse or failure of heavy floor, pre-cast concrete, and steel frame construction	Conduct safe and rescue operations at structural incidents involving the collapse of failure of heavy wall construction	Conduct safe and effective search and rescue operations at structure collapse incidents involving the collapse or failure of light frame construction	Conduct safe and effective search and rescue operations at incidents involving non-structural entrapments and minimal removal of debris and building contents	
Team	Specialty Search and	Conduct High Angle Rope Rescue (including highline	Conduct High Angle Rope Rescue (not including	Conduct Low Angle Rope Rescue		

Collapse Search and Rescue Teams

RESOURCE:				KIND:	Team	
CATEGORY:	Search & Rescue					
MINIMUM CAPABILITIES:						
COMPONENT	METRIC	TYPE I	TYPE II	TYPE III	TYPE IV	OTHER
	Rescue Capabilities	systems), Confined Space Rescue (permit required), and extraction of entrapped victims for Mass Transportation Rescue	highline systems), Confined Space Rescue, and Trench and Excavation Rescue			
Team	Certifications	Confined Space Permit				
Equipment	Technical Search Resources	Same as Type II plus: Audible and optical search equipment to conduct technical search Visual inspection devices Listening devices (seismic and acoustic) Handheld radios	Same as Type III	Same as Type IV plus: Demolition hammers Rotary hammers Hydraulic concrete breakers Hydraulic vehicle rescue system Hammer drill Nail gun Cutting torch Hoisting slings and shackles Rope equipment (kernmantal and lifeline rope, ascenders/ descenders, pulleys, tripod hauling system, carabineers)	Shoring assortment Rebar cutters Reciprocating saws Chain saw Assorted hand tools Generator Lights Extensions cords Air blower Fire extinguishers	
Equipment	Breathing Apparatus	Same as Type II plus: Self-contained (SCBA) Respiratory protection	Same as Type III	Air bags		
Equipment	Medical Materials and Supplies	Same as Type IV	Same as Type IV	Same as Type IV	Medical aid equipment Backboards Stokes stretcher	
Equipment	HazMat Materials and Supplies	Same as Type II	HazMat monitoring equipment Sampling detection kit 4-gas meters Rad monitoring	4-gas meter		

U.S. Department of Homeland Security
Federal Emergency Management Agency

Collapse Search and Rescue Teams

RESOURCE:					
CATEGORY:	Search & Rescue		**KIND:**	Team	
MINIMUM CAPABILITIES:					
COMPONENT	**METRIC**	**TYPE I**	**TYPE II**	**TYPE III**	**TYPE IV**	**OTHER**
			Decontamination equipment 4-gas meter			
COMMENTS:	A State, local, or private technical rescue team that responds to locate, rescue, and recover individuals trapped in a fallen structure or buried in structural collapse.					

FEMA 508-8 Typed Resource Definitions - Search and Rescue Resources
11/14/2005

Mine and Tunnel Search and Rescue Team

RESOURCE:						
CATEGORY:	Search & Rescue (ESF #9)			KIND:	Team	
MINIMUM CAPABILITIES:						
COMPONENT	METRIC	TYPE I	TYPE II	TYPE III	TYPE IV	OTHER
Team	Capability	Inactive or Abandoned Mines or Tunnels	Active mines or tunnels under construction			
Team	Personnel	Same as Type II	8 members (at least 5 qualified on breathing apparatus)			
Personnel	Training	Same as Type II plus: Understanding forces involved in technical rope systems Proficiency in the selection and set up of rescue anchors Ability to construct and operate simple and compound mechanical advantage systems, belay systems and lowering systems Proficiency in technical litter evacuations in a vertical environment	20 hour MSHA initial training on use of breathing apparatus Refresher training sessions underground with breathing apparatus at least every 6 months Use and care of auxiliary mine rescue equipment Mine searching and mapping Mine ventilation procedures and equipment Mine firefighting Any advanced mine rescue training and procedures, as described by MSHA Basic First Aid/CPR			
Equipment	Breathing apparatus	Same as Type II	6 4-hour self-contained oxygen breathing apparatus and a Any necessary equipment for testing such breathing apparatus before putting it into service 1 extra, fully charged, oxygen			

Mine and Tunnel Search and Rescue Team

RESOURCE:						
CATEGORY:	Search & Rescue (ESF #9)		**KIND:**	Team		
MINIMUM CAPABILITIES:						
COMPONENT	**METRIC**	**TYPE I**	**TYPE II**	**TYPE III**	**TYPE IV**	**OTHER**
			bottle			
			6 spare coolant canisters compatible with the breathing apparatus			
			1 oxygen pump or cascading system with portable supply of pressurized oxygen to compatible with the breathing apparatus			
Equipment	Lamps	Same as Type II	10 permissible cap lamps and charging rack			
Equipment	Gas Detectors	Same as Type II	2 gas detectors capable of reading oxygen levels, and any flammable or poisonous gases encountered or anticipated at the rescue location			
Equipment	Communications	Same as Type II	1 portable mine rescue communications system at least 1,000 feet in length			
Equipment	Repair	Same as Type II	Necessary spare parts and tools for repairing the breathing apparatus or communications system			
Equipment	Rigging	Sufficient rope and hardware to support complex rigging				
Equipment	Personal	Same as Type II plus: Full body harness	Head protection compatible with cap lamps Gloves Flame protective outerwear Footwear appropriate to the			

U.S. Department of Homeland Security
Federal Emergency Management Agency

RESOURCE:	Mine and Tunnel Search and Rescue Team			
CATEGORY:	Search & Rescue (ESF #9)		KIND:	Team

MINIMUM CAPABILITIES:

COMPONENT	METRIC	TYPE I	TYPE II	TYPE III	TYPE IV	OTHER
			environment			
Transportation	Resources	Same as Type II	Transportation for all personnel and equipment to mine site			

COMMENTS:

Mountain Search and Rescue Team

RESOURCE:							
CATEGORY:	Search & Rescue (ESF #9)				**KIND:**	Team	
MINIMUM CAPABILITIES:							
COMPONENT	**METRIC**	**TYPE I**	**TYPE II**	**TYPE III**	**TYPE IV**	**OTHER**	
Team	Personnel	Same as Type II	Same as Type III	Same as Type IV	Field team leader Field team members Medical specialist		
Personnel	Navigation Training	Same as Type II	Same as Type III	Same as Type IV plus: Proficiency in back country navigation including: The ability to triangulate a position, ascertain a UTM, utilize GPS, and follow a route to a new location using a topographical map and compass	Navigation (map and compass)		
Personnel	Survival Training	Same as Type II	Operational and technical proficiency in personal survival in mountainous terrain and snow and ice environments	Technical proficiency in personal survival in mountainous terrain and snow and ice environments	Technical proficiency in personal survival in mountainous terrain		
Personnel	Technical Training	Same as Type II plus: Proficient at estimating the mechanical forces involved in technical rescue systems and estimating factors of safety; Proficiency in the use, placement and analysis of mechanical anchors and anchor systems; Proficiency in the use of highlines; Proficiency in the use of slings, etriers, Prusik hitches and mechanical ascenders; Proficiency in the organization and direction of	Same as Type III plus: Understanding of the mechanical forces involved in technical rescue systems; Proficiency in the selection and setup of rescue anchor systems; Proficiency in technical litter evacuation and transport; Litter descents (on steep, vertical, and overhanging rock, on scree and snow, and traversing); Lowering of a subject without a litter; Raising a subject or litter; Knowledge of	Proficiency in bagging, coiling, throwing and storing static and dynamic ropes; Proficiency in tying common knots, and knowledge of their applications and strength efficiencies; Proficiency in search techniques including in hasty and line search techniques, directing line searches, and probe lines			

RESOURCE:	Mountain Search and Rescue Team				
CATEGORY:	Search & Rescue (ESF #9)		KIND:	Team	
MINIMUM CAPABILITIES:					
COMPONENT	METRIC	TYPE I	TYPE II	TYPE III	TYPE IV	OTHER
Personnel	Alpine Training	Proficiency in winter camping in any area, including above timberline; Proficiency in snow and ice climbing; Proficiency in avalanche search and rescue, including recognition of avalanche hazards, avalanche search and rescue organization and leadership, scuff searches, use of SAR dogs; Proficiency in high and low-angle, technical snow and ice rescues and evacuations	procedures involved with helicopter transport Ability to recognize avalanche hazards and to perform avalanche search and rescue including probe lines and avalanche Avalanche awareness training	Understanding of the fundamentals of mountain weather Avalanche awareness training	Basic understanding of mountain weather Ability to walk in mountainous terrain Ability to backpack personal equipment plus one rope at least four miles with an elevation gain of at least 2000 feet Avalanche awareness training	
Personnel	Basic Training	Same as Type II plus: Technical proficiency in one-person rescue and self-rescue techniques Proficiency in mantracking Ability to integrate into and operate using ICS Ability to plan, organize and direct search and rescue missions	Same as Type III plus: Ability to operate using ICS	Same as Type IV	Proficiency in search techniques Awareness of mantracking and maintaining site integrity Understanding of the ICS	
Personnel	Medical Specialist Training	National standard EMT curriculum; ACLS, BTLS	National standard EMT-B curriculum or advanced wilderness first responder; BTLS	Same as Type IV	National standard first responder or wilderness first responder curriculum; BTLS	
Team	Sustained Operations	60 hours	48 hours	24 hours	12 hours	

Mountain Search and Rescue Team

RESOURCE:					
CATEGORY: Search & Rescue (ESF #9)			**KIND:** Team		
MINIMUM CAPABILITIES:					
COMPONENT	**METRIC**	**TYPE I**	**TYPE II**	**TYPE III**	**TYPE IV**	**OTHER**
Team	Rescue Capabilities	Same as Type II plus: Highly trained rescue personnel with multipitch, high-angle experience on vertical rock, ice, and steep snow	Same as Type III plus: Single pitch, high-angle rock rescue	Backcountry, low-angle scree evacuation	Trained rescue personnel with experience in non-technical backcountry evacuation/carryouts	
Team	Search Capabilities	Capable of searching during the day or night. Capable of searching any terrain, including severe rock. Competent IC and section chief	Capable of searching steep, timbered terrain, excluding severe rock, day or night. Competent search team leaders/technicians	Self-sustaining for 48 hours in all weather/terrain, except severe winter/rock	Capable of searching moderate terrain. May be outdoorsmen with basic training	
Equipment	Rescue Supplies and Materials	Same as Type II plus: 8-10 ropes of various lengths (200-400 ft)	Same as Type III plus; 6-8 ropes of various lengths and a full complement of rescue/climbing gear	Same as Type IV plus: 4-6 ropes of various lengths	Harnesses; Helmets; Basic hardware; Rope; Radio communications on a common frequency	
Equipment	Search Supplies and Materials	Equipped to be self-sustaining for 60 hours in all environments; Radio communications on common frequency	Equipped to be self-sustaining for 48 hours in all environments; Radio communications on common frequency	Equipped to be self-sustaining for 24 hours in all weather/terrain, except severe winter/rock	Equipped to be self-sustaining for 12 hours in all weather/terrain, except severe winter/rock	
Equipment	Personal Supplies and Materials	Same as Type II plus: Food for 60 hours	Same as Type III plus: Water container of two-liter capacity and/or quantity of water appropriate for the conditions. Food for 48 hours. Second light source	Same as Type IV	Appropriate clothes and footgear for both fair and foul weather; Water container of 1-liter capacity and/or quantity of water appropriate for the conditions; Day pack; Five large, heavy-duty plastic trash bags; Food for 24 hours; Headlamp or flashlight; Lighter, matches and candle, or equivalent waterproof fire source; Knife; Compass;	

FEMA

U.S. Department of Homeland Security
Federal Emergency Management Agency

RESOURCE:	Mountain Search and Rescue Team				
CATEGORY:	Search & Rescue (ESF #9)		**KIND:**	Team	

MINIMUM CAPABILITIES:					
COMPONENT	METRIC	TYPE I	TYPE II	TYPE III	TYPE IV	OTHER
					Personal First Aid Kit; Waterproof pen/pencil and paper; Whistle; Two pairs plastic or vinyl examination gloves	
Equipment	Medical Supplies and Materials	Same as Type II	Same as Type III	Same as Type IV	As appropriate for level of training, as applied in wilderness environment and meeting local protocols and requirements	

COMMENTS: Search for and rescue people in trouble either above the timberline or in high-angle areas below the timberline, which can include glacier, crevasse, backcountry and alpine search and rescue, and educate the population in safe activities so they will be able to avoid the dangers that result in the need for rescue.

Definitions

GPS	Global Positioning System
Navigation	The practice of charting a course for a group of people (team) using basic tools such as a map and compass.

RESOURCE: Radio Direction Finding Team

CATEGORY: Search & Rescue (ESF #9) **KIND:** Team

MINIMUM CAPABILITIES:						
COMPONENT	METRIC	TYPE I	TYPE II	TYPE III	TYPE IV	OTHER
Personnel	Team members	Team leader and team members to support at least 2 operational field units (at least 1 team member must be a medical specialist – EMT or higher) Management staff following ICS model	Team leader and team members to support at least 2 operational field units Management staff following ICS model	Team leader Team member(s)		
Personnel	Crew Availability	Same as Type II	Available for more than 1 full day of operations	Available for at least 1 full day of operations		
Personnel	Training	Must be able to operate the team's equipment Team is expected to be able to triangulate a distress beacon to its source Team members must be experienced in coordinating with other search teams and aircrews Team members must have training for operations in remote locations for extended periods One member of each team must have advanced medical training to the EMT level	Must be able to operate the team's equipment Team is expected to be able to triangulate a distress beacon to its source Team members must be experienced in coordinating with other search teams Team members must have training for operations in limited remote locations for extended periods	Must be able to operate the team's equipment Team is expected to be able to triangulate a distress beacon to its source in moderate terrain Team members are not expected to operate in remote field locations for extended periods		
Vehicle	Transportation	4x4 vehicles that can transport each team throughout the search area	Vehicles that can transport each team throughout the search area 4x4s are not required, but recommended	1 vehicle that can transport the team throughout the search area 4x4s are not required, but recommended		

RESOURCE: Radio Direction Finding Team

CATEGORY: Search & Rescue (ESF #9) **KIND:** Team

MINIMUM CAPABILITIES:

COMPONENT	METRIC	TYPE I	TYPE II	TYPE III	TYPE IV	OTHER
Equipment	Clothing	Same as Type II	Same as Type III	Appropriate level of PPE for working environment		
Equipment	Communications	Same as Type II	VHF Radios Cell Phone	Cell Phone		
Equipment	Electronic	Same as Type II	At least one Handheld Portable Electronic Direction Finder per team	At least one Handheld Portable Electronic Direction Finder		
Equipment	Rescue	Equipment to support remote extrication and field transport of aircraft crash survivors	None required	None required		
Personnel	Overhead Incident Management	Same as Type II	Incident staff capable of managing electronic direction-finding operations	Unit level mission release No search management capabilities		

COMMENTS
Team members will usually only work a maximum of 12-hour shifts, depending on individual unit policies and procedures.

Crew availability does not require continuous availability of specific personnel, only that crews are available to those specifications.

Medical support and technical rescue equipment is expected to be provided by local EMS for Type II and III teams.

Swiftwater/Flood Search and Rescue Team

RESOURCE:	Swiftwater/Flood Search and Rescue Team				
CATEGORY:	Search and Rescue		**KIND:** Team		
MINIMUM CAPABILITIES:		**TYPE I**	**TYPE II**	**TYPE III**	**TYPE IV**	**OTHER**

COMPONENT	METRIC	TYPE I	TYPE II	TYPE III	TYPE IV	OTHER
Personnel	Team Composition	14 member team 2 managers 2 squad leaders 10 personnel	6 member team 1 squad leader 5 personnel	4 member team 1 squad leader 3 personnel	3 member team 1 squad leader 2 personnel	
Personnel	Minimum number Technical Animal Rescue	2	1	1		
Personnel	Minimum number ALS Certified	2				
Personnel	Minimum number Helicopter/ Aquatic Rescue Operations	4	2			
Personnel	Minimum number Powered Boat Operators	4	2			
Personnel	Minimum number SCUBA Trained Support Personnel with Equipment	4	2	2		

RESOURCE:		Swiftwater/Flood Search and Rescue Team				
CATEGORY:	Search and Rescue			KIND:	Team	
MINIMUM CAPABILITIES:		TYPE I	TYPE II	TYPE III	TYPE IV	OTHER
COMPONENT	METRIC					
Personnel	Number and level EMTs	14 EMT - B 2 EMT - P	Same as Type III	Same as Type IV	1 EMT - B	
Team	Sustained operations	Same as Type II	24-hour operations	Same as Type IV	18-hour operations	
Team	Capabilities	Manage search operations Power vessel operations Helicopter rescue operational Animal rescue HazMat ALS Communications Logistics	Manage search operations Power vessel operations Helicopter rescue operational Animal rescue HazMat BLS	Assist in search operations Nonpowered water craft Animal rescue HazMat BLS	Low-risk operations Land-based HazMat BLS	
Team	Specialty S&R Capabilities	Same as Type II	Same as Type III plus: Technical rope systems	In-water contact rescue Dive rescue		
Team	Training	Same as Type II except:: Divers to have 80 hours of formal public safety diver training	Same as Type III plus: Helicopter operations Awareness Technical rope rescue	Same as Type IV plus: Divers to have 60 hours of formal public safety diver training	Class 3 paddle skills Contact and self-rescue skills HazMat ICS Swiftwater rescue technician	
Team	Certifications	ALS Advanced First Aid & CPR	Same as Type IV	Same as Type IV	BLS Advanced First Aid & CPR	
Equipment	Transportation Resources	Equipment trailer; Personnel support vehicle				
Equipment	Communication	Same as Type II	Same as Type III plus: Aircraft radio	Same as Type IV plus: Headset	Batteries Portable radios	

Swiftwater/Flood Search and Rescue Team

RESOURCE:

CATEGORY: Search and Rescue

KIND: Team

MINIMUM CAPABILITIES:						
COMPONENT	METRIC	TYPE I	TYPE II	TYPE III	TYPE IV	OTHER
					Cell phone	
Equipment	Medical	ALS medical kit Blankets Spineboard Litter	Same as Type III plus: Spineboard	Same as Type IV plus: Litter	BLS medical kit Blankets	
Equipment	Personal	Same as Type II	Same as Type III: plus: Life vests HEED except: PFD Type V	Same as Type IV plus: Fins Lamps	Flares; Markers; Bags; Flashlight; Gloves; Helmets; Light sticks; PFD Type III/IV; Knives; Shoes; Whistles	
Equipment	SCUBA	Same as Type III	Same as Type III	SCUBA cylinder Buoyancy compensator Weight belt 2 cutting tools Chest harness & snap shackle Full face mask U/W communication Dry suit Search line Spare SCUBA cylinder		
Vehicle	Rescue Boat	2 - Fueled	1 - Fueled	1 - Non-powered 4 person		
COMMENTS	Conduct search and rescue operations in all water environments including swiftwater and flood conditions. Water rescue teams come with all team equipment required to safely and effectively conduct operations. For a complete listing of recommended training, skills, and equipment, please reference the FIRESCOPE Swiftwater/Flood Search and Rescue definition at: http://www.firescope.org/ics-usar/ICS-SF-SAR-020-1.pdf.					

RESOURCE:	US&R Incident Support Team				

CATEGORY:	Search & Rescue (ESF #9)	KIND:	Team		

MINIMUM CAPABILITIES:					
COMPONENT	METRIC	TYPE I	TYPE II	TYPE III	TYPE IV	OTHER
Personnel	Number of People per Response	30-60 depending on the needs of the incident	22			
Personnel	Training	Same as Type II	Qualified National US&R Response System			
Personnel	Areas of Specialization	Provide staffing to fill all necessary ICS functions to the assigned incident Provide technical assistance in the acquisition and utilization of ESF #9 resources through advice, Incident command assistance, Incident response planning, Management and coordination of US&R task forces Obtaining ESF #9 logistical support	Provide staffing for 14 ICS functions activated to provide technical assistance in the acquisition and utilization of ESF #9 resources through advice, Incident command assistance, Incident response planning, Management and coordination of US&R task forces Obtaining ESF #9 logistical support			
Personnel	Sustained Operations	24-hour operations for a minimum of 14 days before requiring personnel rotations and can provide administrative and living support if necessary	Type II is an advanced element of Type I Will require supplemental IST staff to perform 24-hour operations rotations			
Personnel	Organization	Fully staffed US&R multi-functional management team; Organized based on ICS guidelines, Command and Command Staff and Operations, Planning,	Organized based on ICS guidelines, Command and Command Staff and Operations, Planning, Logistics, Finance and Administration			

FEMA

US&R Incident Support Team

RESOURCE:

CATEGORY: Search & Rescue (ESF #9) **KIND:** Team

MINIMUM CAPABILITIES:

COMPONENT	METRIC	TYPE I	TYPE II	TYPE III	TYPE IV	OTHER
		Logistics, Finance and Administration				
Equipment		Same as Type II	Living support as necessary			
Supply	Computer Supplies	Same as Type II	Ink cartridge; CD; Computer; Disk; DVD; Modem; Mouse; Mouse pad; Printer; Scanner			
Equipment	Communication Equipment	Same as Type II	Antennas; Celwave; Fax; GPS; Microphone; Pager; Phone; Radio; Repeater; Receiver; Recorder; Repeater; Satellite; Satellite phone; Speaker phone			
Equipment	Tools	Same as Type II	Blade; Can opener; Chisel; Drill; Drill bit; Fire extinguisher; Flashlight; Guywire; Hammer; Handtruck; Knife; Level; Lightstick; Measuring tape; Nails; Paint; Pump; Rope; Shovel; Screwdriver; Smoke detector; Saw; Wrench; Toolkit; Tool bag; Wire brad; Wrecking bar; Wrench			
Equipment	Power Supply	Same as Type II	Battery; Bulb; Charger; Electric cord; Extension cord; Generator; Grounding; Power adapter; Power cord; Power supply; Socket; Surge protector; Transformer; Watt meter			
Supply	Administrative	Same as Type II	Accounting book; Acetate; Binder clip; Chalk; Chalk line Bracket; Calculator;			

RESOURCE: US&R Incident Support Team

CATEGORY: Search & Rescue (ESF #9) **KIND:** Team

MINIMUM CAPABILITIES:

COMPONENT	METRIC	TYPE I	TYPE II	TYPE III	TYPE IV	OTHER
			Clipboard; Envelope; Etcher; FEMA logo; Filing box; Flip chart; Folder; Form; Glue; Handbook; Hole punch; Laminating sheets; Letter tray; Marker; Marker-board; Measuring tape; Memo pad; Name tag; Note pad; Paint; Paper; Paper clip; Pen; Pencil; Push pins; Rubber band; Ruler; Scissor; Sheet protector; Shrink wrap; Sign; Stamp; Staple; Stapler; Staple remover; Stationery; Stenopad; Tape; Tape dispenser; Three hole punch; White out; Writing pad			
Equipment	Logistics	Same as Type II	Can opener; Cleaner; Clock; Cup; Garbage bag; Road atlas; Tissue; Toilet paper; Zip-lock bags; A/C unit; Blanket; Chair; Commode; Cot; Fan; MRE; Pillow; Sheet; Sleeping bag; Sleeping pad; Table; Tarp; Tent; Towel; Water			

COMMENTS Federal asset. ISTs provide Federal, State, and local officials with technical assistance in the acquisition and utilization of ESF 9 resources through advice, incident command assistance, management and coordination of US&R task forces, and obtaining ESF #9 logistic support. ISTs are self-sufficient and mobilize within 2 hours of a request.

US&R Task Forces

RESOURCE:							
CATEGORY:	Search & Rescue (ESF #9)		KIND:				
MINIMUM CAPABILITIES:		TYPE I	TYPE II	TYPE III	TYPE IV	OTHER	
COMPONENT	METRIC						
Personnel	Number of People per Response	70-person response	28-person response				
Personnel	Training	Same as Type II	NFPA 1670 Technician Level in area of specialty Support personnel at Operations Level				
Personnel	Areas of Specialization	High angle rope rescue (including highline systems) Confined space rescue (permit required) WMD/HM operations Defensive water rescue ALS intervention Communications	Light frame construction and basic rope rescue operations HazMat conditions Trench and excavation rescue ALS intervention Communications				
Personnel	Sustained Operations	24-hour S&R operations Self-sufficient for first 72 hours	12-hour S&R operations Self-sufficient for first 72 hours				
Personnel	Organization	Same as Type II	Multidisciplinary organization of Command; Search; Rescue; Medical; HazMat; Logistics; Planning				
Equipment	Sustained Operations	Same as Type II	Potential mission duration of up to 10 days				
Equipment	Rescue Equipment	Same as Type II	Pneumatic Powered Tools Electric Powered Tools Hydraulic Powered Tools Hand Tools				

RESOURCE:	US&R Task Forces				
CATEGORY:	Search & Rescue (ESF #9)		**KIND:**		
MINIMUM CAPABILITIES:					
COMPONENT	**METRIC**	**TYPE I**	**TYPE II**	**TYPE III**	**TYPE IV**	**OTHER**
			Electrical Heavy Rigging Technical Rope Safety			
Equipment	Medical Equipment	Same as Type II	Antibiotics/Antifungals; Patient Comfort Medication; Pain Medications; Sedatives/ Anesthetics/Paralytics; Steroids; IV Fluids/Volume; Immunizations/Immune Globulin; Canine Treatment; Basic Airway; Intubation; Eye Care Supplies; IV Access/ Administration; Patient Assessment Care; Patient Immobilization/Extrication; Patient/ PPE; Skeletal Care; Wound Care; Patient Monitoring			
Equipment	Technical Equipment	Same as Type II	Structures Specialist Technical Information Specialist HazMat Specialist Technical Search Specialist Canine Search Specialist			
Equipment	Communications Equipment	Same as Type II	Portable Radios; Charging Units; Telecommunications; Repeaters; Accessories; Batteries; Power Sources; Small Tools; Computer			
Equipment	Logistics	Same as Type II	Water/Fluids; Food; Shelter; Sanitation; Safety;			

US&R Task Forces

RESOURCE:					
CATEGORY:	Search & Rescue (ESF #9)			**KIND:**	
MINIMUM CAPABILITIES:					
COMPONENT	**METRIC**	**TYPE I**	**TYPE II**	**TYPE III**	**TYPE IV**	**OTHER**
	Equipment		Administrative Support; Personal Bag; Task Force Support; Cache Transportation/Support; Base of Operations; Equipment Maintenance			
COMMENTS	Federal asset. There are 28 FEMA US&R Task Forces, totally self-sufficient for the first 72 hours of a deployment, spread throughout the continental United States trained and equipped by FEMA to conduct physical search and rescue in collapsed buildings, provide emergency medical care to trapped victims, assess and control gas, electrical services and hazardous materials, and evaluate and stabilize damaged structures.					

RESOURCE:		Wilderness Search and Rescue Team			
CATEGORY:	Search & Rescue (ESF #9)		**KIND:** Team		
MINIMUM CAPABILITIES:					
COMPONENT	**METRIC**	**TYPE I**	**TYPE II**	**TYPE III**	**TYPE IV**	**OTHER**
Team	Rescue Capabilities	Same as Type II	Backcountry, low-angle evacuation	Same as Type IV	Trained rescue personnel with experience in nontechnical backcountry evacuation/carryouts supported by local technical experts	
Team	Search Capabilities	Capable of conducting self-sustaining full search operations for 72 hours in all weather and low-angle wilderness terrain Competent and experienced Incident Command staff	Capable of conducting self-sustaining full search operations for 48 hours in all weather and low-angle wilderness terrain Competent and experienced Incident Command staff	Same as Type IV	Capable of searching high-probability local wilderness terrain for short durations (24 hours or less)	
Personnel	Team Composition	At least 6 team leaders and 48 team members to support at least 6 operational field units (at least 1 member of each team must be a medical specialist – see below) Management staff following ICS model	At least 4 team leaders and 28 team members to support at least 4 operational field units (at least 1 member of each team must be a medical specialist – see below) Management staff following ICS model	At least 2 team leaders and 6 team members to support at least 2 operational field units Must be supported by local EMS and technical rescue personnel	At least 1 team leader and 3 team members Must be supported by local EMS and technical rescue personnel	
Personnel	Medical Specialist	National standard EMT curriculum; ACLS, BTLS	National standard EMT-B curriculum or wilderness first responder; BTLS	Same as Type IV	Not required – supported by local EMS	
Personnel	Overhead Incident Management	Same as Type II	Incident staff capable of managing wilderness search operations	Same as Type IV	Unit level mission release No search management capabilities	
Personnel	Crew Availability	Same as Type II	Available for more than 1 full day of operations	Same as Type IV	Available for at least 1 full day of operations	

Wilderness Search and Rescue Team

RESOURCE:						
CATEGORY:	Search & Rescue (ESF #9)			**KIND:** Team		**OTHER**
MINIMUM CAPABILITIES:		**TYPE I**	**TYPE II**	**TYPE III**	**TYPE IV**	
COMPONENT	**METRIC**					
Personnel	Sustained Operations	72 hours	48 hours	Same as Type IV	24 hours	
Personnel	Training	Same as Type II plus: Personnel demonstrate proficiency in mantracking and working with expert mantrackers	Same as Type III plus: 1 member of each team must be current to the requirements of the medical specialist (see above Must also be knowledgeable of procedures involved with helicopter transport and coordination with search crews, both ground and air Must have the ability to operate in an ICS structure, and be able to plan, organize, and direct search and rescue missions Team members must have training for operations in remote locations for extended periods	Same as Type IV plus: Proficiency in backcountry navigation (including the ability to triangulate a position, ascertain a UTM, use GPS, and follow a route to a new location using a topographical map and compass) Must be proficient at conducting and directing search lines	Must be able to operate the team's equipment; Team members are not expected to operate in remote field locations for extended periods Must have basic navigation training using a map and compass Must have technical proficiency in personal survival in local wilderness terrain Must have awareness of mantracking and maintaining site integrity Must have a basic understanding of the ICS Must have proficiency in hasty search techniques	
Vehicle	Transportation	4x4 vehicles that can transport each team throughout or to the search area	Vehicles that can transport each team throughout or at least to the search area 4x4s are not required, but recommended	Same as Type IV	1 vehicle that can transport the team throughout or at least to the search area 4x4s are not required, but recommended	
Equipment	Clothing	Same as Type II	Same as Type III	Same as Type IV	Appropriate level of PPE for working environment	
Equipment	Communications	Same as Type II	Same as Type III plus: VHF capability to	Same as Type IV plus: VHF communications	VHF Radios for team communications	

RESOURCE:	Wilderness Search and Rescue Team				
CATEGORY: Search & Rescue (ESF #9)			**KIND:** Team		
MINIMUM CAPABILITIES:					
COMPONENT	**METRIC**	**TYPE I**	**TYPE II**	**TYPE III**	**TYPE IV**	**OTHER**
Equipment	Search & Rescue	Same as Type II	communicate with aircraft	capability with other teams	Cell Phone	
			Equipment to support remote extrication and field transport of survivors	None required	None required	
Supply	Self-sustaining	Equipped to be self-sustaining for 72 hours in local wilderness environments	Equipped to be self-sustaining for 48 hours in local wilderness environments	Same as Type IV	Equipped to be self-sustaining for 24 hours in local wilderness environments	
Equipment	Medical	Same as Type II	Same as Type III, plus ability to support survivors	Same as Type IV	As appropriate for level of training, as applied in wilderness environment and meeting local protocols and requirements for support of the team	
COMMENTS	Team members will usually only work a maximum of 12-hour shifts, depending on individual unit policies and procedures. Crew availability does not require continuous availability of specific personnel, only that crews are available to those specifications, though some personnel may have extended assignments in the field. Medical support and technical rescue equipment is expected to be provided by local EMS and other technical rescue personnel for Type III and IV teams.					

www.ingramcontent.com/pod-product-compliance
Lightning Source LLC
Chambersburg PA
CBHW080635290526
45790CB00007B/3068